to

M000074146

Carmen Warrington is an accomplished performer, meditation artist, songwriter and vocussionist. (The term 'vocussionist' was coined for her blend of rhythmic and percussive words and sounds.) Carmen has a degree in psychology, and is a graduate of the National Institute of Dramatic Art. She has written and recorded top-selling meditation CDs and cassettes, and is a member of the internationally acclaimed jazz-fusion band AtmaSphere. Through her business 'Calm and Creative', Carmen runs workshops which focus on creativity and meditation for professional artists and people who simply want to experience and develop their innate artistic talents. *Today I Will ... meditations to make your life calm and creative* is available on CD through her website at www.calmandcreative.com.au

CARMEN WARRINGTON

today I will...

100 ways to make your life calm and creative

Lothian
BOOKS

Thomas C. Lothian Pty Ltd
132 Albert Road, South Melbourne, Victoria 3205

National Library of Australia
Cataloguing-in-Publication data:

Warrington, Carmen.
    Today I Will ... : 100 ways to make your life calm
    and creative.

    ISBN 0 7344 0238 4.

    1. Self-help techniques. 2. Affirmations. I. Title.

158.1

Designed by Kim Roberts Design
Back cover photograph by Lynette Zeeng
Colour reproduction by Scott Digital, Port Melbourne
Printed in Singapore by Craft Print International Ltd

acknowledgements

I have been fortunate to meet hundreds of inspiring people; thank you all for sharing your discoveries and realisations with me, and for shaping my thinking. I express my deep thanks to: the Brahma Kumaris World Spiritual University for teaching me to meditate and for guiding me on my journey towards love and light; my mother and father, my sister, Lisa, and my brother, Jan, for nurturing my creative spirit, and teaching me so many virtues; and all my fantastic friends who enthusiastically supported this book, and who have always believed in me — especially Pamela and Chrissy. Thanks to Kim whose design breathes life into each page. My eternal thanks to David for his loving kindness. And my unending gratitude to the Source of All Inspiration.

Introduction

I have always loved peace. When I am calm and my mind is peaceful I experience love, contentment and inspiration; I feel connected to others and I can cope with whatever challenges come my way. In 1984 I took up meditation, and it was a turning point in my life. To feel at peace while meditating is a wonderful thing; to feel that same inner peace while going about my day — relating to people, dealing with the situations that make up my life — is a great adventure.

We are all blessed with a creative spark — the key to our personal growth. We have a wealth of knowledge available to us about the soul, the mind and the subconscious, which can help us to reach our true potential. To achieve this, we only need to keep this intention in mind, and recognize the opportunities life presents us.

I hope you enjoy these activities, and they bring you greater self-awareness through calmness and creativity. Meditations to accompany *Today I Will* are available on CD from my website.

today I will...

The language we use colours our experience. Strive to use expressive words today, and avoid words such as *nice*, *good*, *great*, *okay*. Express your truths more colourfully.

flavour my conversation with vibrant words and expressions.

Why downplay your experiences with ordinary words? Heighten your perceptions and live a rich and vivid existence.

today I will...

Write yourself a note or find an image of peace, and keep it near you. Between tasks think *peace*. Before and after a phone call think *peace*. While walking about, visualise peace emanating from you. When you interact with others imagine your peace influencing the atmosphere.

keep reminding myself that I am a **peaceful** soul.

You don't need to search for peace; you are a peaceful being. If you don't feel peaceful you have forgotten this truth. Remind yourself of your peaceful nature again and again.

today I will...

create a map of my

Draw, paint or make a collage of your life and chart the major events, relationships and choices. Include the obstacles (mountains), the ebb and flow of life (rivers), periods of growth, stability and stagnation (forests, gardens, swamps) and major decisions (crossroads). Depict times of strong emotions as weather patterns. Let your imagination guide you and enjoy the process.

ourney through life.

Take a refreshing new look at your history. Tune into the rhythms and cycles of your life. See clearly where you have come from and where you are going.

today I will...

Set aside time, make yourself comfortable, turn up the music and really listen. Use headphones to lose yourself in the music without disturbing anyone. Let music enter your soul and open yourself to this rich experience.

feed my soul with music to lift my spirits.

Music inspires, soothes and energises. Music guides you to reflection, reminiscence and daydreams. Music fills you with energy, enthusiasm and optimism. Music heals the soul.

today I will

write a list of acts of love.

To help you compile your list, recall actions that expressed your love, and the acts of love others have shown you.

Love means so much more than sex or romance. Keep alive the greater meaning of the love we all seek. Recognise the love you give, and cherish the love you receive.

today I will

uplift the atmosphere.

Do you complain about the weather, what life has dealt you, your health, other people, the government, or the system? Clear thinking leads to change, but complaint usually leads nowhere.

Complaints sap energy, and drag others down. Instead of complaining find ways to radiate energy. Be the one to uplift the atmosphere.

today I will...

Even if you feel as though you are having one of the worst days of your life, you have reasons to be grateful. Look for the benefit in all that has happened to you. Put things into perspective. You are alive! Focus on what you have.

be grateful for all my life's blessings.

We are frequently undermined by a state of hungry discontent. Appreciate the gift of life and all its wonders.

today I will...

dance through my day

On Monday have you already begun to wish it was Friday afternoon? Many activities and chores are routine and repetitive — approach them with spirit and gusto. Whether you work to earn an income or maintain a household, remember that all work can be an act of love and gratitude.

o the music of enthusiasm.

The secret of enthusiasm: if you put more energy into your activities you become energised. Enthusiasm overcomes tiredness. Treasure each precious moment of your existence. Inject the atmosphere with positivity.

today I will...

take the role of peacemaker and

Do you feel resentment towards another? Do you want to punish them or teach them a lesson? Ask yourself if you are willing to resolve this conflict. Are you sure they started it and that they should finish it? These are signs that you are unwilling to resolve the conflict.

onsider resolving a conflict.

Unless you are willing to reach a resolution the conflict will remain. Uncover the attitudes which prevent you from making peace. In conflict there is always a solution — if you really want to find one. Be the one who takes the first step towards peace.

today I will...

Stop everything mid-morning and take two minutes to savour deep peace. Take the phone off the hook, close your eyes and retreat from the world to the still, silent centre of your mind.

refresh my soul
with two minutes of silence
or meditation.

Keep your life in perspective by remembering who you are and what is important to you. Bring your inner peace to the world through your activities and interactions.

today I will...

The choices and decisions you make shape your future.
What is right for another person may not be right for you.
Practise the art of tuning in and trusting yourself.

listen to the whisperings
of my intuition.

Sometimes we make decisions based on what we expect of
ourselves, or what others expect of us. Your intuition is your sixth
sense about people and situations and sometimes it can seem
illogical or without reason. Trust your inner voice and enjoy the
fruits of your choices.

today I will

donate to a worthy cause.

Choose an organisation or charity that has a special meaning for you. Go without one or two little treats for a week and donate the money, or offer your time.

Connect to a greater sense of community. Giving to those in need helps you to recognise and give thanks for the abundance in your own life.

today I will

send a thank-you note to a friend.

Express how this friendship enhances your life. Highlight something they did for you or said to you. Tell them how they support or inspire you.

Show your appreciation for the gift of friendship. Cherish what you share together.

today I will...

Do you compare yourself to other people? Do you rank yourself better or worse than others according to your appearance, your job, your possessions, your friends, your talents and skills, your gender, or your intelligence?

treasure myself
as a unique soul.

Most of us focus on our imperfections. As a reaction, and to protect ourselves, we transform these feelings of inadequacy into the belief that we're better than everyone else. In truth we are all equally valuable. Override your doubts and insecurities. Repeatedly affirm today that you are unique, there is no one like you.

today I will...

write my life as a story,
beginning with

First, decide whether you will write your story as an adventure, a fairytale, a myth, legend, detective yarn, or science fiction. Paint the people in your life as vivid characters. Start at your birth, and let significant events present themselves. Invent an end for your story.

Once upon a time...'

This is a wonderful way to make sense of your life's journey so far, to identify themes and to seek a greater meaning for significant events.

today I will...

Whatever your addiction is — cigarettes, coffee, chocolate, a pattern of behaviour — you will need 100 per cent determination and preparation. Organise alternatives to help cope with withdrawal and ask for help if necessary. Focus on making it through the day. Addictions allow us to avoid or suppress feelings, so look for clues to your deeper issues.

give up one of my little addictions — just for one day.

Exercise your willpower. Become strong, independent, free. If you can manage it for one day, why not try giving it up again tomorrow … just for one day.

today I will...

let my light shine by listing al

Relax and let go of your resistances. Recall praise you have received. Ask yourself questions to unlock your hidden treasures. What am I good at? What are my strengths and special attributes? What can people rely on me for? How do I make others happy? What do I like about my nature, my spirit? How have I overcome challenges? What is at the heart and soul of me?

ny best qualities and virtues.

Focus on the good in you and watch it grow. Life is easier with self-respect as your foundation. Remember to see the positive qualities in others too.

today I will

ask for help.

Perhaps you expect too much from yourself. Or feel uncomfortable asking for assistance? Even if the person you ask can't help you, help will come. Life is supportive, though not always in the way we expect.

Great things are achieved through the power of co-operation. We are not alone, and we benefit from giving and taking.

today I will

delight in making a gift with my hands.

Draw a picture, pot a plant, make a toy, give a foot massage, sew, invent a new dessert, decorate something, or make greeting cards. Perfection is not necessary. Give your gift from the heart and complete the circle of love.

Let your loving intentions permeate your creation. It is definitely the thought that counts. Gifts you make are priceless.

today I will...

If you had all the money and resources and support networks you could possibly wish for, what would you do? Given the money, resources and supports that you have now, what would you do? What would you say to people you love?

plan what I'd do with my life if I had only three months to live.

You're not rehearsing for life — this is it! Live every precious moment of it.

today I will...

Boost someone's confidence through positive feedback —
motivate, inspire, give courage, remove doubts. Reassure them
of their capacity to succeed. Praise them for their efforts. Play
the role of mentor.

empower someone through words of encouragement.

Encouragement is an easy form of giving. Rather than doing a
task for someone, encourage them to do it for themselves.

today I will...

remember what I was like as

Look at photos from your childhood. Share your feelings and
anecdotes of childhood with a friend. Ask your parents,
grandparents or siblings what they remember about you.

child and compare

myself now.

Who you were as a child is very important. Your childhood dreams
and wishes come from the very core of you. The growing up
process can separate you from your essential nature. Reconnect
with who you were when you came into the world.

today I will...

Close your eyes and imagine your perfect sanctuary. Make it exactly as you wish, paying attention to the ambience, the fragrances, textures, light and location. It can be a natural setting such as a cave or a forest, or a structure that you visualise. Arrange significant objects or talismans in your sanctuary.

visit my inner sanctuary.

Retreat to your sacred place, where you are completely safe and can be true to yourself. Connect with your spirituality — examine your soul and seek answers to your deepest questions, or just be.

today I will...

set the table with my finest ware
an everyday mea

Bring out your best tablecloth and favourite crockery. Decorate the table with candles and flowers. Play some beautiful music. Pay attention to table manners. Eat a little more slowly. Perhaps ask your companions to dress for the occasion. Leave the cleaning up till later.

nd transform
nto a special occasion.

Give all your senses a treat. Savour your meal and take pleasure in the grace, elegance, peace or conversation of the occasion.

today I will

immerse myself in art.

If you can't visit a gallery, studio or museum, you can delve into art books, greeting cards, posters, photographs, sculpture and architecture. Or search through the art section of a secondhand bookshop.

Absorb the art, its colours, shapes, textures, beauty and impressions. Open yourself to new perspectives, and allow yourself to feel strong emotions. Remove yourself from high-tech, logical society for a while and retreat to the visual world of art.

today I will
claim my right
to nurture myself.

Take a bubblebath, have a massage, cook yourself a special meal, read your
favourite poetry, meditate, potter, or do something nice for yourself.
Tell yourself you deserve to be nurtured. Give your desires a high priority
in your day.

Enjoying a good quality of life is just as important as fulfilling your
responsibilities. Keep a balance between expending and replenishing
your energy. Treat yourself well and enjoy life.

today I will...

It is rare for anyone to be entirely blameless. Is your share of the blame lost in a long chain of events and reactions? Perhaps you have forgotten. Search your heart. Sometimes it helps to understand that mistakes are really just poor choices. Once you have accepted this, you might have the courage to heal a relationship.

admit to myself that I could have been partly to blame.

Own your part in the matter and stop the situation recurring. Heal past wounds. End the habit of blaming others and be free to learn and grow.

today I will...

Give your young advisor enough information to form an opinion. You don't have to follow their advice, but do give it your honest consideration.

have the humility to ask a younger person for advice.

A younger person may have a simpler approach to life, or a more adventurous one. Or they may see the bigger picture. Their opinion will help you step out of your comfort zone and try something new.

today I will...

Allow five to ten minutes for this creative meditation. Imagine you are swimming in an ocean, being tossed by the waves. Create the experience as vividly as you can by concentrating on each of your senses. Then let yourself sink down slowly under the water (where you can still breathe normally). Enjoy drifting weightlessly in the pleasant coolness. Rest a while, floating, immersed in the still, silent water, until you are ready to return to the surface.

dive into the ocean of peace.

Experience tranquillity in your busy day. Revitalise and refresh yourself in an ocean of peace.

today I will...

Find out the other person's needs rather than assuming you know them. The easiest way is to ask. Then identify your own needs. If you *always* give up your own needs for the sake of others, you undervalue yourself.

put another person's needs before my own.

Conflict arises when your needs are different to another's. Peace is possible when you accept that everyone's needs are important. Give and take are both valuable. Be flexible and generous today.

today I will

explore the chemistry of my body and mind.

Keep a journal of what you eat and drink for one day. Monitor your energy levels, physical reactions, mental clarity, and moods.

You are affected by what you ingest. Small refinements and adjustments to your eating habits can make a big difference to your health and wellbeing.

today I will

be patient.

Be prepared for things to go wrong. Make allowances for the fact that other people have different rhythms to you. Slow down your thoughts. Breathe more deeply. There are many challenges to patience in a single day.

There is a season for everything and you cannot rush it. By mastering patience you are caring for your health. With less anxiety you will enjoy each day.

today I will...

Between activities stop for half a minute of peace, take a few deep breaths, stretch and look at something in the distance. Do this before the next conversation, before you pick up the phone or begin the next task. Make space for what is to come. Reflect, and allow your head and heart to catch up.

float tranquilly between tasks.

Be more efficient and tranquil. Relax amid activity. Create mental space. Enjoy frequent retreats into timelessness.

today I will...

Paint or draw your feelings, or make a collage. Don't rely on your logical self; feel free to be abstract. Symbols, doodles and stick figures are all acceptable. This creation is for you alone, to express your feelings safely. Capture images from your dreams or meditations.

give shape, size and colour to my feelings.

Repressing or suppressing your feelings is unhealthy. Access feelings that you may not be able to articulate in words yet. Reveal a deeper part of yourself through imagery, the language of the subconscious mind.

today I will...

Are you dissatisfied with how you look? Is your self-esteem too bound up in your physical appearance? Love your body; it is the extraordinary instrument through which your spirit expresses itself. Accept the inevitability of ageing. Broaden your concept of beauty.

accept what I see
in the mirror.

Be at peace with yourself as you let go of impossible self-imposed standards. Live in the present, not in the past (how you used to look) or the future (how you will look when you find time for more exercise).

today I will...

give recognition to the peopl

They may be writers and philosophers, family members who have loved you unconditionally, people who have taught you by their example, role models who have inspired your personal best, or anyone who has shaped your thinking.

who have influenced my life.

Balance your overactive ego. Credit is due to many people for your achievements and virtues. Your ideas are born from all the ideas that came before. And remember, you also influence others.

today I will...

Learn to be tolerant and easygoing. Tolerate behaviour and mannerisms that normally irritate you. Remain unaffected by sharp words, thoughtlessness, selfishness and inflexibility. Accept the ways of drivers and pedestrians. Forgive the manners of your customers, colleagues and superiors.

become a calming influence in the world and radiate peace.

Overcome the habit of reacting. Soften your hard edges.

today I will

compose my own wise saying.

Imagine you are famous and a reporter is interviewing you. What have you learnt that you would like to share with the world? Give your unique perspective on life. No one else will have experienced life quite like you.

See the greater significance of incidents and events in your life. Celebrate the lessons life has taught you by distilling your experiences in a piece of insight or wisdom.

today I will

creatively seek solutions.

To solve a problem take yourself to a contrasting environment — if it's a work-related issue go to a cafe or park. Describe the situation to yourself in the third person, as though you are talking about someone else. List every possible solution, even the wild and outrageous ones. What advice will you give your best friend — yourself?

Step back from your worries. Observe yourself and your circumstances to make your issues and options clear.

today I will...

Use massage oil or cream on your hands to press, squeeze, rub, rotate and smooth. Keep the pressure firm and gentle. You could also swap a massage with a friend or lover.

nurture myself by gently massaging my feet, hands or head.

The nerve-endings for the whole body, all the organs, internal systems and energy meridians finish at the feet and hands. Tune up your whole system. Relax and energise.

today I will...

Visualise doing something you're fearful of, and ask yourself what the worst outcome could be? Now imagine the worst that could happen if you don't face this fear. Have faith — overcoming obstacles will make you stronger.

courageously look fear in the face.

Fear can save us from life-threatening situations, but sometimes fear denies us life-affirming new adventures. Don't be afraid to move forward. Acts of courage are rewarded.

today I will...

celebrate life by filling an empt

Pick a few flowers from your garden for a small vase. Or buy a flower arrangement that suits your budget. You don't need to spend much to feel wealthy. If you don't have a vase, use a bottle, mug or teapot.

pace with fragrant flowers.

Decorate a table or bedside cabinet with fresh flowers to delight your senses and uplift your soul. Get in touch with nature, its complexity and its purity. Why wait for a special occasion when every day is precious?

today I will

meditate on a virtue.

Which virtue can help you best today: humility, clarity, courage, perseverance, honesty, flexibility? While you meditate, imagine the virtue is a tiny ball of light within you growing bigger and brighter. Visualise yourself as the embodiment of this virtue in your life.

Increase your virtues to live a beautiful life. Be the best you can be. Tap into your unlimited potential.

today I will

simply let go.

It's great to be in control, and it's great to let go. Let go of your expectations and fixed ideas about how things should be done. Don't try to force things to happen. Just do as much as you can, then step back and see what takes shape. If you feel responsible for someone else's moods or emotions let these feelings go.

Relax and allow new influences and options to emerge. Let your destiny steer you.

today I will...

Repeat the question over and over. Write or speak each of your answers aloud. Remain constructive and positive. The phrase, 'I am the one who...' will lead you to a new perception of yourself. Perhaps you will answer the next question, 'Why am I here?'

deepen my self-awareness by answering the question, 'Who am I?'

Discover new aspects of yourself and voice them. Glimpse your true self and your purpose in life.

today I will...

How well do you listen? Do you let others finish speaking before you begin to talk? Give people who are talking to you your full attention, without judging them or giving them advice. Make eye contact. Listen in order to understand. Allow more time for people who reply in few words. Ask questions when appropriate.

cultivate the art of listening.

Listen to others the way you would like them to listen to you. We have a basic need to be heard and understood. Disagreements between people arise because of misunderstandings or assumptions. Build a rapport and harmonise your relationships.

today I will

be independent, innovative and unique.

Don't let the opinions of others influence you. Whose life are you living? Free yourself from caring about what other people think. What do *you* think? Being an individual is one of the greatest gifts you can give to your community.

Opinions about what you do and how you do it will always abound. Feel at ease with yourself. Stand up and be counted.

today I will

give something away.

Pass on an item you no longer use or give away an object you value highly.

Creating an empty space invites the new. You do not truly own anything, so practise being a trustee of your possessions. Be generous and have faith that you will receive what you need.

today I will...

resist the urge to gossip or tal

Do you want to waste your life talking negatively about others? Work out in advance what you will say to counter gossip. For example, 'Can we deal with this some other way?' Or 'I'd rather only say things to their face.' Be prepared for others to try to undermine your attempts.

bout someone behind their back.

Relationships thrive on trust and respect. How would you feel if you knew people were gossiping about you? It takes courage to reject such a powerful and destructive habit.

today I will...

Just do one thing at a time. Keep your mind on your actions and talk to yourself about what you're doing. Involve all your senses in each activity. If your thoughts wander bring them back to the present.

live in the present and focus on what I am doing.

Have you ever forgotten to lock the front door, left the iron on, or forgotten where you put your wallet? Be present in every second of your day. Feel at peace, make fewer errors and experience the richness of each moment.

today I will

set a course for my future.

Make a list of your goals, both short-term and long-term. List personal as well as career goals. Focus on the big picture — look at *what* you want to achieve rather than *how* you plan to achieve it. With your goals in sight, you can choose wisely which path to follow.

With a destination in mind your journey through life has focus and purpose. You can choose to use your energy and resources in worthwhile ways by asking the question, 'Does this path take me closer to my goal?'

today I will

slay the dragon of habit.

Step outside your comfort zone. Walk up the stairs instead of taking the elevator; accept a new responsibility; take a risk.

We become creatures of habit too easily. If you do what you've always done, you'll get what you always get. Don't let life pass you by — get out of the rut.

today I will...

Say something significant in conversation — a thank you or an encouragement. Be understanding, patch up a quarrel, or spend a few extra moments in gentle exchange before getting down to business.

treat others as though I will never see them again.

Getting a task done is important and so is making a little extra effort to connect with people. Remain free of regret.

today I will...

We all seek harmony. Communicate your feelings. Before you speak, choose the right environment, and rehearse what you want to say. Be open and honest. Work out how far you are prepared to go in the interests of good relations, then go a step further. Be generous and good-hearted.

clear the air of a misunderstanding.

A small skirmish can escalate into a major battle. Address misunderstandings immediately to conserve energy, prevent conflict and enhance your relationships.

today I will...

You may know someone's essential nature, but you'll never know all the details of their life. Ask them about their first love, their greatest adventure, their most profound lesson in life, or their latest plans.

discover something new about someone I love.

Keep your relationships fresh, and avoid making assumptions, or taking each other for granted. Enjoy moments of inspired intimacy.

today I will...

learn a wise saying, inspiring

The key to learning is repetition. The more times you read or reflect on the words to a poem or song the easier they are to recall. Study the words so their meaning is clear, and link them to pictures in your mind.

poem or song lyric by heart.

Choose a song or piece of writing that resonates with you — it's likely to be something you need to tell yourself (or another) in challenging times.

today I will

tune in to synchronicity.

Contact someone you've been thinking about. Thoughts do travel to their destination. When you think of someone it is likely they are thinking of you.

Cultivate a subtle understanding — learn to read the signs. Go where you are guided. Follow your hunches and act on your impulses.

today I will

be punctual.

The key is planning. Allow extra time in your preparations to dress appropriately, and check you have the address. Remember, even locking the door, catching the elevator and walking to the car take time.

To arrive early or right on time is a sign of respect. Reduce your stress levels and avoid causing inconvenience to others. Settle yourself before an appointment, and focus on your reasons for being there. Prepare to encounter obstacles, and resolve any strong emotions.

today I will...

This is the greatest alchemy! Each of us learns about life at our own pace, through our own experiences. Instead of condemning another's choices put yourself in their shoes. They have good reasons for their choices and the lessons they need to learn are not yours.

transform my unkind thoughts about another person.

Thoughts reach their target so take care. You cannot change anyone else; you can only change yourself.

today I will...

centre myself by

Counting slowly to three, breathe in through your nose.
Then hold for another three counts. Breathe out through your
mouth for a count of five or eight — pause and repeat.
Breathe deeply so the air expands your lower ribs rather than
your upper chest.

reathing deeply for five minutes.

Relax and unwind from the tensions of the day. Energise your
mind and body, and calm your nervous system. Centre yourself.
Take a step back from the day's events and allow yourself to
recover from any strong emotions.

today I will...

Take the phone off the hook and go somewhere private. You may choose to listen to music that inspires you.

luxuriate in candlelight and dream.

Use this time to create new dreams, review recent events, tune in to your creative centre and refresh your energy. Enjoy solitude and unstructured time. Retreat to your peaceful centre and renovate your soul.

today I will...

Think before you speak and choose your words with care. In conversation, listen carefully to others so you don't go over what has already been covered. Try eating in silence. Renounce all unnecessary banter today and conserve your energy. Let people around you know your intentions beforehand so they won't take offence.

spread peace by speaking less.

You are a peaceful soul. Experience your inner peace and refresh your mind in silence.

today I will...

free myself from the subtle

Perhaps the unfinished project is no longer relevant or necessary, or has been given a much lower priority. Decide if the project is still worth investing your energy in and, if not, put it to rest once and for all.

chains of an
unfinished project.

Is the cause of your procrastination fear or confusion? Invoke the appropriate virtue or power needed to complete the task. You are a powerful soul.

today I will

reminisce over old photos.

Be prepared for emotional reactions; from joy about the good old days to melancholy for the loss of loved ones. Allow your feelings to arise without blocking them, and connect with your feelings about your life now.

Appreciate the people and events in your life. Honour the past, and see how you've evolved.

today I will

engage more fully
with people.

Make every effort to be absolutely present in the company of other people. Use eye contact and give them your undivided attention. Include a little personal communication in every exchange. Greet a passer-by, chat to strangers in a queue, or smile at someone in an elevator.

Value every interaction — it is how we experience love. There is nothing more important.

today I will...

Write continuously for three pages. Simply start writing and allow your thoughts and feelings to surface. Continue writing without worrying about grammar, or trying to edit your words. Don't plan what you'll write, or pause to read over the pages until you've finished the third page.

bring my inner world to light.

Make time for reflection. Each day brings new experiences and the way you respond to those experiences creates your attitudes, habits and personality. Stay in control of your life through regular reflection and self-inquiry.

today I will...

Why write someone off because they have done something mean-spirited or made a mistake? Embrace all the shades of their personality and behaviour. You have inconsistencies too. Be kind and generous with your judgements.

accept that people are inconsistent.

Build relationships that endure. Let go of resentments. Be at peace with yourself and the world, and learn to love unconditionally.

today I will...

recognise the smal

An achievement can be as simple as doing a task well, bouncing back after a disagreement, or following a routine all week. Self-encouragement is the key to self-esteem.

chievements
        I have made recently.

Praise yourself for small achievements to create a feeling of success. As you feel more successful you'll become more daring. Focus on the things you do well and you will thrive.

today I will...

reach out to someone with

Is this person on another wavelength? Do you seem worlds apart? Ask them what their passion in life is to lead you into a deep conversation.

whom I do not have an easy rapport.

You may discover you have completely misjudged or underestimated someone. Find out what makes their flame burn brightly and be awe-inspired by the world's glorious diversity.

today I will

rearrange part of my material world.

Rearrange your desk, your drawers, photos, pot plants or furniture —
experiment! If it's a shared space, get everyone's agreement before you start.
There'll be tidying and cleaning involved, so allow time for it.

Make a change. Spark up a stagnant space. Shift energy blocks. Set a new
rhythm in motion.

today I will

replenish my energies in nature.

Walk, sit under a tree, visit a garden, sit by water, watch a sunset, breathe the fresh air and let the breeze caress your face. Get in touch with the elements.

Ground yourself. Absorb life-energy from nature. Reconnect with the seasons of your life.

today I will...

keep a calm perspective.

Allow five to ten minutes for this creative visualisation.
Imagine your body is a cloud — insubstantial, misty, ethereal.
Sense the lightness of your being. Let your cloud-self rise and
float through the roof, beyond the treetops and up into limitless
sky. Look down on your building, your street, your town. As you
float higher, look down at the Earth. You see our planet, with its
billions of inhabitants, each a precious member of your world
family. Stay there for a few moments, enjoying the feeling of
weightlessness. You are one small part of a huge interconnected
community. Slowly and gently float to Earth and return to
your body.

today I will...

Use your own poetic structure, rhyme and grammar and no one else's. Let the poem evoke a moment in time, a person, an event, an impression or a feeling. Put yourself in a creative space and indulge in the intensity of the experience. This poem is for you alone.

write a piece of poetry for myself.

Live in full and exquisite colour. Find the sacred in the ordinary. Give a voice to the deep and meaningful part of yourself. Rejoice in your insights.

today I will...

Consider the possibility that your way of doing things is not the only way. Other methods may be just as valid. Think about how you want the chores to be completed, your opinions about what makes good driving, or the way you communicate. Consider deeply your personal rules — are they so essential that everyone should do the same?

wholeheartedly embrace alternatives.

Acquire tolerance, become less set in your ways, learn to adapt and be in harmony with others rather than trying to control them. Respect alternative points of view.

today I will...

Imagine you've been asked to speak at a special occasion in celebration of someone else's life. Invite others to help you compile the list. Write their virtues out beautifully to make an uplifting gift.

make a list of someone else's best qualities and virtues.

Instil in yourself the habit of seeing the best in everyone. Focus on the positive and help others to be the best they can.

today I will...

Notice how many times you put yourself down during the day. Include what you think and say, and words spoken in jest. Pay particular attention to how you react to your mistakes and poor choices. Think of yourself as a child who is learning to walk; you need encouragement — not criticism.

affirm positive messages about myself.

You will become the person you believe you are. Affirm positive messages about yourself. Treat yourself gently and with respect. You deserve it.

today I will

sit in a different
chair at home.

If you intend using someone else's favourite chair, ask their permission first.

We are such creatures of habit. This simple choice allows you to see things from a different angle. Break old patterns and habits, and discover new perspectives.

today I will

make repairs.

You could choose to repair clothing, household items, toys, tools or a vehicle. If you really can't fix it, consider replacing it.

Things left in disrepair are a slow and steady drain on your subconscious. To fix or discard something broken is an energy-cleanse for you and your household.

today I will...

Whatever happened cannot be changed; it is now part of your history. Your past has shaped you and brought you to this moment. Cast from your mind phrases such as 'I should have', 'why didn't I' and 'if only'. Accept the lessons you have learnt from past choices. Make peace with yourself.

put a full stop on the past.

Disentangle yourself from regret, shame and guilt. Shake off the past and move forward with peace of mind.

today I will...

Honour your innermost thoughts and feelings and bring them forth into your full awareness. Ask yourself if you are being the most loving person you can be.

connect with my true feelings about others.

Is this really what you think and feel, or have you adopted the habits of your family or friends? Dare to be you. Learn to be less critical and judgemental, and become more loving and kind.

today I will...

acknowledge that I am doing

From time to time there will be circumstances that are beyond your control. It's important to recognise and accept this fact and stay calm. Sometimes all you can do is just hang in there. Everything changes in its own time.

he best I can right now.

Break the cycle of self-criticism. Curb your desire for perfection, and be reasonable about what you expect of yourself. Become compassionate and understanding of yourself and others.

today I will...

144

Breathe deeply, and slow down your thoughts. Take a break. Re-schedule. Ask for an extension on a due date or deadline. It's not the end of the world if one deadline is missed, especially if the deadline is self-imposed.

give myself permission to relax and take it easy.

Lower your stress levels. Realise that there is enough time to do whatever you want in your day, your week, and your life.

today I will

let kindness motivate me.

Show kindness to others without expecting thanks or praise in return. Be selfless. You have so much to give. Be a benefactor. Offer your services without being asked.

Open your heart and your life to new opportunities. The laws of the universe are fixed principles, and when you give you are bound to receive. Feel good about yourself.

today I will
relieve neck and shoulder tension.

Taking several short breaks to stretch during the day can do wonders. Stretch, extend, rotate, tighten then release muscles. Check your posture and unclench your jaw. Take three deep breaths. Mentally let go of stress and tension. Relax for two minutes.

Avoid pain and headaches, as well as the long-term damage stress can cause. Allow blood to flow more freely to your brain. Give your eyes a rest. Energise your mind and body.

today I will...

Pick up litter, recycle, use your own shopping bag, and buy environmentally safe products. Write letters to manufacturers and producers urging them to take more responsibility for the environment, or join an environmental group.

devote my energy to being a guardian of the environment.

Your contribution counts and you will inspire others to care.

today I will...

In the midst of criticism we deny, blame and close off. Feel secure in the knowledge that you are being guided towards your highest potential. Remember, it is not your whole self being criticised. If the criticism has some basis, welcome the chance to polish the rough edges of your character.

seek the truth
in some criticism of me.

It takes courage to face your own shortcomings, and the rewards are freedom, relief, self-respect and the opportunity to improve.

today I will...

Use a large piece of paper and coloured pencils, pens, crayons or Textas, chalks or paint. One person starts by drawing on the page, and then the other responds. Abstract shapes and squiggles are all part of this language. Don't speak while your conversation takes place on the page. Talk about your experience afterwards.

communicate with a friend by drawing pictures.

Non-verbal communication accesses a different and creative part of you. Rediscover each other in delightful ways.

today I will...

regard obstacles and upheaval

Carefree times are wonderful, but wouldn't life be dull if nothing ever changed? When a challenge comes along assume you are ready to deal with it. Instead of asking why it is happening, accept the opportunity to grow and to become more powerful.

s opportunities for spiritual growth.

Obstacles and upheavals are opportunities to fine-tune your soul. Seek a deeper significance in events. Look for life's lessons.

today I will...

value people whose nature

Reverse the tendency to belittle or criticise those whose nature is the opposite of yours. To overcome your frustration with them, acknowledge how they complement your shortcomings. If your talent is to see the big picture, who pays attention to the small details? Dynamism is balanced by gentleness, frankness by subtlety.

s the opposite of mine.

Diversity is nature's survival mechanism. Imagine if the whole world was exactly like you. The contrasts and differences between us give rise to creation and invention. Embrace the differences in others and increase your capacity for love and acceptance.

today I will

simplify my life.

The list of things you have to do is always growing. On the day you die there'll still be things you haven't finished, so why push yourself so hard? Be realistic with your list of things to do and see if you can halve it, or at least reduce it.

Make the enjoyment of a good quality of life the most important item on your list. Lower your stress levels. Take the pressure off.

today I will

go for a pleasure walk.

Visit a new location and absorb the shapes, colours and aromas. Notice sounds nearby and afar. Appreciate the expanse of sky and let your eyes focus into the distance. Enjoy the physical sensations of your limbs and feet at work in perfect co-ordination. Clear your mind of complex thoughts.

Be simple. Enjoy mingling your senses with the elements. Give your mind a rest, release unwanted moods and lighten your spirit. Be tranquil.

today I will...

Credit or praise someone in private, acknowledge them in a meeting, or put a congratulations note on the fridge door. Create a fortnightly award ceremony in which everyone is a winner.

honour the small achievements of those around me.

This is an uplifting experience for everyone. Usually the big things are given so much focus, but saying thank you honours our countless small achievements, which often go unnoticed.

today I will...

Phone or write your apology if a face-to-face apology feels too challenging. If you want to apologise to someone who has passed away, picture them in your mind, or focus on a photograph of them while you speak.

lighten my heart by making an apology.

Let go of shame, guilt or regret; they hinder your growth, and keep you trapped in the past, stuck in self-hatred. It is time to move on and heal. Restore equality in an important relationship.

today I will...

practise the virtue

Let your judgement of others — strangers, friends or family — be tempered by compassion. Even people you know well have mental or emotional struggles you cannot fully comprehend. We all seek peace and happiness. All our actions and all our choices are made to achieve this end, although what motivates us may not be clear to an onlooker.

of compassion.

Seek to understand others rather than condemn them. Know that they are doing the best they can in completely different circumstances to yours.

today I will...

Look at your priorities and see if you can drop the least important items to free up your resources. The stronger your reasons for saving, the more ways you will find to save.

plan ways to save money, time or energy.

Make yourself more efficient. You can afford it. There is time. Take charge of your life. Create the opportunities to fulfil your dreams.

today I will

accept others as they are.

Why waste time and energy trying to change someone else's behaviour? Perhaps you are the only one who wants them to change. The only person you have the power to change is yourself. Adapt, be flexible, and adjust your expectations.

Changes in yourself will impact on those around you, and may be a catalyst for changes in them too, but don't *expect* them to change.

today I will

follow my passion in life to the full.

What is your passion in life? Make sure you have given it a high priority. Ask yourself if you really need so many possessions, or whether you must do the household chores constantly. Do you feel as though your life is slipping by? Make time for yourself.

Do you work in order to live, or live in order to work? Life is about more than merely survival. If you don't take action now — then when?

today I will...

write a letter to someone I an

Use this safe method to let off steam, rather than lashing out at someone. Do you believe people who say they never feel angry? Uncover hidden resentments and disappointments in yourself. Air your grievances and voice your needs on paper.

angry with and then destroy it.

Reacting angrily is harmful, even dangerous, but suppressing anger can cause feelings of depression. Over time, as you learn to voice your needs to others, your anger will have less power over you.

today I will...

send healing thoughts to

Remain positive and caring. Detach yourself from the sadness surrounding events in the news. Be grateful that you are safe, and use your heart and mind to serve others. Imagine yourself as an angel caring for traumatised souls with your loving and silent presence.

rouble spots around the world.

Thoughts and good wishes reach their intended destination. When it's not possible to be physically present, you can still lend your help and support.

today I will...

Observe what causes you stress and anxiety. Visualise ways of overcoming or preventing your stress reactions. Either remove the stressors from your life or learn to change your responses. Often our attitudes and thoughts cause us stress. Make sure your solutions to stressful situations are realistic, achievable and uplifting.

devise five ways to make my life calm.

Peace is the foundation of happiness and fulfilment. Peace is your natural state. You are a calm and creative being.